TWO TREES
—in the—
GARDEN

Spiritually Nourishing Poetry

Stephen McKee

WESTBOW
PRESS*
A DIVISION OF THOMAS NELSON
& ZONDERVAN

WestBow Press books may be ordered through booksellers or by contacting:

WestBow Press
A Division of Thomas Nelson & Zondervan
1663 Liberty Drive
Bloomington, IN 47403
www.westbowpress.com
1 (866) 928-1240

ISBN: 978-1-5127-3772-1 (sc)
ISBN: 978-1-5127-3773-8 (e)

Library of Congress Control Number: 2016905842

Print information available on the last page.

WestBow Press rev. date: 4/11/2016

CONTENTS

FOREWORD

I had the distinct pleasure of discovering the poetic styling's of Mr. Steve McKee back in 2012. It was with no small amount of trepidation that I ventured into an online forum dedicated to both readers and writers of poetry. These poets wanted to share their thoughts and to read the thoughts of others, receive feedback from their peers and, in general, mingle with other people who understand what it is like to need poetry in your life. To my great joy, I found myself surrounded (cyberly speaking, of course) by a world full of like-minded poets. Steve McKee was one such writer.

Mr. McKee's words stood out to me immediately. His gentle deliverance of various topics, along with his free flowing form, offers a balm that can calm the mind and lift the soul. I delved into his numerous poems with fervor and found a kindred spirit. From humor to sadness, from wizened lessons to spiritual mentoring...Steve's poetry spoke to me in a way that few others have. Within the shared thoughts of this wonderful human being I have found moments of peace, self-speculation and much wisdom. He has brought to me numerous smiles and even a few gut-clutching laughs. Steve McKee's poetry transcends the idea of traditional poetry. He speaks and writes from his heart and in so doing...captures the hearts of his readers. As many poets do, Steve sees the world through his own eyes...and then shares his vision in words. However, his viewing and sharing has the ability to uplift and to make others reflect internally on a deeper level.

In 2012, I had the immense pleasure of working with Steve (along with fellow poet and mutual friend, Nick Hayward) on another publication of the heart, *Poetic Synergy*. Our combined efforts led to not only a book that I am extremely proud to have been part of, but also to a deep and abiding friendship. I truly believe that God places you in the presence of certain people and circumstances at just the right time of life when you need them most. Mr. McKee is an invaluable friend and mentor. I thank God for using our mutual love of poetry to ensure that I was in the right time and place to benefit from such a person; from such a God given talent as he.

In the following pages, you will find yourself on a journey through the mind of a wonderful modern day poet. I hope that you find his words as inspiring, uplifting and as internally reflective as I have. With a talent that most certainly is a gift from a higher being, I truly believe that there are words and thoughts given here that will minister to each and every person that will read.

"There are the people who walk the skies and report what they observe. There are the people who show us what it is to live and how to die. There are the ones who lift us up with every word and as they do, we choke and lose the will to speak and feel the tears go down our cheek."
~ The Poet and the People ~ Steve McKee

Steve, you are one of those "people".

Evangeline King
Co-Author, Poetic Synergy

To
To my brother Albert
You remind me of Jesus,
the First born of my forever family.

INTRODUCTION

"In the beginning, God created the Heavens and the Earth". From that time until now Science and Religion have done a lot to muddy the water and obscure the truth. The same pride that got Lucifer expelled from heaven afflicts those of us who inherited his sinful nature. With everyone stirring the pond, there is rarely an opportunity to cast an objective glance in God's direction.

We have a nature that demands food, rest and entertainment, yet in these things, there is no lasting satisfaction to be had. Many of us have found that there is lasting nourishment and rest in a relationship with God. We turn aside from the appetites that seek control over us and find peaceful rest beside God's still waters. This all occurs because something very special has taken place. The people of God have come to this place because they have yielded their lives to the control of God's Spirit and received forgiveness for their sin by virtue of the death and resurrection of God's Messiah, Jesus.

The objective of love is not to be proven right or to prove someone else wrong. The objective of love is to love. How do we know who to love? God has admonished us to love everyone. He has not told us to impose our will upon them. Jesus said, "By this all men will know that you are my disciples; that you have love for one another." Concerning what we have to say, Peter wrote, "always be ready to share a reason for the hope that lives within you".

In the poems I offer, it is my hope to present God given ideas, devoid of contentions opinion. If you discover contention or evidence of human pride, it is my fault. If you encounter God, it is by His design and loving grace. May you be blessed and nourished.

TWO TREES IN THE GARDEN

Once again we return,
seeking that which we may learn,
though this path has been taken
with ambitions long forsaken.

Still we come and still we eat
and yet we leave so incomplete.
Every path has been well traveled
as our world comes all unraveled.

Back to the tree of knowledge;
Perhaps another year in college.
Hopeful verses, same sad song;
seeming right but going wrong.

There are two trees in the garden.
One will soften, one will harden.
One will give you life abundant;
the other pain and loss redundant.

Man most often chooses death.
It's in his eyes, it's on his breath.
Though this fruit is so attractive,
The deadly toxin is still active.

Having chosen knowledge solely,
The toxin enters killing slowly;
causing bitterness inside
as it's victim swells with pride.

Final death by strangulation
comes with no anticipation.
Always right and ever proud
all dressed up in Satan's shroud.

There are two trees in the garden.
One will soften, one will harden.
Why is one the tree of choice?
Is there perhaps another voice?

What of the wondrous Tree of Life
that feeds eternal without strife?
There are two trees in the garden.
One brings death, the other
pardon.

SPAWNING

"Why Jesus?" you ask; "why is He different?"
In discussions concerning religion, that
question is asked a lot and rarely answered
to the satisfaction of the one asking.

The answer can be discovered in self.
The world we live in and the doctrine it
propagates is in essence selfish.
Jesus, in all He was and is, is selfless.

The bible says, unless a corn of wheat
goes into the ground and dies, it remains
by itself alone, yet in its death it is multiplied.
Jesus came to earth to die.

Millions of women and men speak of their
right to choose and millions of babies die.
The mother salmon sacrifices her own life
in order to spawn generations of her kind.

Spawning involves going against the current
and following an inborn purpose, that's what
Jesus did and that's what His people are supposed to do.
That is simply, "Dying to self" and trusting God for life.

Until you are armed with that purpose,
given you by God's spirit, you will be selfish.
Selflessness becomes more evident as people
continue on the same path Jesus walked.

As near as I can tell, everyone else promotes religion.
Jesus is not about religion, He is about people.
He died so that many would experience eternal life.
As we die to self, others experience the aroma of that life.

THE PROPHET WILL SPEAK

The prophet will speak in these days we are in.
Pray that we hear as his words cut the air.
What now comes to be, before never has been.
Though his words some despise, we should heed what is there.

The dimming's begun and the day is far spent.
Though the curtain comes down, still the veil is pulled back.
As believers abandon this house we've been lent,
all evil makes ready it's final attack.

Through all that is coming to terrify many,
our God in His Son, will still keep us quite safe.
Our hearts should be broken for those with no haven,
who've chosen so wrongly the enemies' gate.

HOME

And so, we are here for this bit of time
to learn of the value of tears and of pain.
To show us the value of light hearted laughter;
to value hard work under sunshine or rain.

After coming home tired all the years we've been given,
we treasure the love that waits inside the door.
There is blended for us the sweet nectar of Heaven.
Still from light, there's a shadow says we have to have more.

Still, home is the fortress that calls us, "come hither",
with riches abundant, with peace love and light.
Still waiting for us, the sweet nectar of Heaven
and each time we taste it, there's savored delight.

With eyesight that's dimming and worn aching bodies
we've learned to appreciate sips slowly measured.
While Home is the fortress that calls us, "come hither"
and Heaven's the name of the home we now treasure.

A FEW QUESTIONS

What distance is traveled by spirits in shadows
who escape from the flesh that once kept them bound?
Are they here very near us while away with their Maker
and are we fleshlings able to know they're around?

What is it in us that separates beings by
physical/spiritual as we come and we go?
Is there not more to living than the pain and the dying?
Is it not all connected and doesn't it flow?

Are these questions the source of the fear and the longing
that battle it out in the depths of our souls;
and if there are questions are there not also answers
from the One who controls how eternity rolls?

CANDLE POWER

Are you someone who lights candles
or are you someone who blows them out?
Are you an extinguisher of hopes and dreams
or do you encourage as you visualize their fulfillment.

If there is any light, anywhere,
darkness cannot prevail.
If there is real love anywhere
then hatred has no power.

Life, Love and light are one
and bring God's bounty to the human soul.
They are the power over death,
hatred and darkness.

Light, Life and love prevail for eternity.
Death, hatred and darkness will surely end.
May we all choose the warmth and light of Love
and not the cold bitter darkness of hatred.

THE PROUD, THE FEW

A few token words,
left as manna for wondering peasants.
They won't understand but they will
learn to despise their own ignorance.

The great ones always share
and those lesser beings learn of
their station on this crowded orb.
Being wretched can be such fun.

We are all so different.
Some must be greater and others lesser.
Some looking down and most looking up.
The down lookers supposing they are being looked up at.

CONNECTED

Is there not much gladness to be had,
at someone else's being glad
and how much joy does one receive,
when some other one believes?

We are all Humans being
Loving, living...hearing seeing.
Inexorably connected;
some accepted, some rejected.

To quantify the worth of each,
is out of any mortal's reach.
Still, there is loss and there is gain
and ministry of joy and pain.

May we each love and value other,
stranger, friend or sister, brother.
May we be light along the way
and shine, in all we do and say.

IN THE CLOUDS

In the clouds, whether standing or walking,
I encounter others and wonder at their Godlike ways.
As it happens, I wonder, "how is it I am here with these?"

In the clouds, whether strolling or resting,
there is a preternatural sense of beings and surroundings.
I am delighted beyond words to be here, now with such.

In the clouds, whether thinking or doing,
I know I am being acclimatized for Heaven.
I love all that are here with me and envision us out of our cocoons.

In the clouds, we all have time for all.
The light and mist provide and we feed on each other's words.
How close are we now? How much closer will we be?

A CAUSE TO DIE TO

If you have the Savior,
you have the Holy Spirit.
If you have the Holy Spirit,
you don't need a cause.

Every day you are appointed
will come to you in its time.
On that day, you will have choices
to make in the course of your journey.

God is there for you inside
and he will pilot your vessel;
Through storms as well as calm waters,
it is no longer you who lives but Christ.

Religion offers you standards and goals,
Jesus simply offers life eternal.
The greatest gift ever given is simply that;
a gift, bought and paid for and freely given.

Jesus doesn't need us. We need Him.
He has provided oneness with the Father
through His unselfish love and grace.
His love flows into and through all who are His.

If you are tired of searching...stop.
He will provide rest, peace and joy.
If you are lost in your sin...cry out.
He will hear you and end your nightmare.

Jesus said, "I am the Way, the Truth and the Life.
No man comes to the Father but by Me."
A lot of religions have causes.
People who have new Life....have Jesus.

NO LONGER CONTAINED

Having once again plateaued after ascending to a
new understanding of purpose and mission,
I look around at this ethereal environment
and once again recoil at the idea of achievement.

I am here, because I have found my way through
the many days that are mine by Sovereign grace.
I wake in the morning and do what I find
as One greater than I works me into His plan.

There is no arriving here for me or by my hand.
There is no getting that is not quicksilver.
There is no one for me to convince or change.
There is only the purpose that is new every morning.

It is unknown to me, as I am only a stone.
The Master Mason works His will and shapes me.
Some of the shaping is painful but there isn't
a lot of pain as I was chosen for my shape originally.

He works, I live/and have built in purpose.
He speaks and I hear the voice of a King
in my own private chamber.
I have my place in the wall; in His city.

There are many others like me and we share.
Some of us are so powerfully connected.
We are side by side or above or below in the wall.
We are unable to explain the place of blessing we have.

Love strengthens the wall as we share it.
The Builder has arranged it all so meticulously.
This wall is not confining, rather it sets us free.
We are larger than we know and no longer contained
in time or space.

ETERNAL WONDER EVER NEW

When the wonder is long worn,
it is again new.
As it seems the day dims,
the light of another dawns.

The brush soft rhythm of ever,
obliterates the idea of never
and love again dresses us up
for another lovely day.

TODAY LORD

May there be healing today
as we all go our way;
healing from bitterness, envy,
resentment and the sickness they bring.

May there be joy Lord I pray
as we keep to your way;
The joy of Salvation and Your
Families companionship that makes a heart sing.

May there be love Lord today
we can share on the way;
with our brothers and sisters
who to You and each other so desperately cling.

May there be strength Lord today
and confidence in Your great provision.
May we all, as your children,
run and take flight as though on Eagle's wings.

GRACE

What an existential dichotomy.
We teach selfishness to our children
and then express our annoyance when
we encounter it in others.

We call people to account for
the very things we are guilty of
and speak of their need for
the fortitude to become what we are not.

In all of this we ignore the
only true answer to all of our afflictions;
Grace, God's grace; channeled through
its recipients to others.

No one meets the standards set by
either God or man, though God is right.
The difference is, God recognized man's
deficiency and did something about it.

We leave and forsake, when God doesn't.
We demand perfection, when God provides it.
We let our anger and disappointment guide us,
when God is Himself guiding, dependable love.

This world is in a death spiral as are
the people who refuse to believe God.
Those who do believe have come to terms with
their wretchedness and are in Ascension.

When we see the symptoms in others and
know them for what they are, we patiently
administer the only available antidote.
Truth, spoken in compassionate love.

That is Grace

THOUGHTS ON BEING BLESSED

How blessed to have loved
and to have been loved;
to have breathed life's
most fragrant air and
to have lived.

What privilege is had
in being, knowing and doing;
in adjustments made and
failure's turned into success,
having achieved.

What light is given us,
illuminating our path
by others who give it
without knowing what
we have received.

What great security is
there, while on the wheel
shaping continues on
through finishing touch
of the Potter's hand.

BEING GATHERED

May I look into His face in confident anticipation
as this life's last breaths are softly drawn
and break the plane to God's forever nation,
where there is no more death and Life goes ever on.

Then I will arrive and have my glad forever,
knowing blessed reunion with all who've gone before.
No more sadness, pain or difficult endeavor.
With all supplied, I'll have no need of more.

King Jesus will embrace me; hold me in His loving arms
as we begin a journey without end.
I will know as I've been known as we continue on,
and have a great forever, with my dearest friend.

As this dark world is gladly left behind me
and the light and joy of Heaven take me in,
there will be no valid reason to remind me
of this place so sad and compromised by sin.

TAKE THE GOLD

God has extended an invitation to anyone
to believe and have His life forever.
Having been told this, many ask, "why does
God allow this thing or that?"
The answers to those questions and more
exist in His eternal nature.
He is offering that nature to mankind;
free to us but at considerable expense to Him.
Still, convinced of our right to question God,
we pursue endless questions and irrelevant
issues that mask our own need.
Eternal life has nothing to do with time
but everything to do with quality and nature.
A person who accepts God's offer is for the
rest of his or her life on earth, given God's
nature and personal presence. For that same period
that person converses with God and experiences
His companionship. When one leaves this earth,
all of the barriers come down and the believer
knows fully what was previously only known in part.
So, you ask, "how is it you know this?"
The only answer there is, is this; I know this
from having known the God of the Universe
personally for over fifty years. In that time,
He has revealed Himself and His truth to me.
Here is the question I have for you.
If I were to offer you a million dollars in Gold,
would you ask me about my previous performance
or would you take the gold?

SOMETIMES, THE SUN RISES
IN THE EVENING

Sometimes, the sun rises in the evening
when people take time to step out of the parade
and draw near each other, seeking riches
of a greater sort than the world's cheap currency.
There is a warming at the consumption of
Heaven's rich and flavorful nectar and a unity
that refuses human boundaries.
What mountain perch offers such a vantage point;
What conveyance a more thrilling transportation?
No dollar, mark, shekel or yen compounded at any
rate of interest will purchase the evening sun.
For those of us who take time to touch and love,
sometimes, the Sun rises in the evening.

THE WELL

How many times have you been to this well
and drunk until you could no more.
Although much was consumed, still nothing is there
and futility is all that you know.

Desperate longing and searching go on
for that something that all will fulfill;
There is thirst in each soul for
a sip that provides complete satisfaction.

There is one who waits by just such a well
and offers the water of life.
He bids, come drink your fill and
know the peace and freedom provided.

No contamination, no false promises or disappointment,
only fulfillment and calm from no more need.
Come, all who thirst and receive the
authentic water of life.

PORTAL

"Let's get your coat and shoes on",
his mother prompts in warm singing tones.
He goes out to play.

He moves with alacrity toward the swing set
and selects his favorite swing.
She watches in secret from the window.

He grips the chains and pumps to gain
speed and elevation and notices his
mother at the window.

A grin and a wave for mommy
and he pumps ever harder.
Even through the window, they are one.

He is not a mathematician or
a neurosurgeon, he is just a boy.
Still .... he is a wonder.

The window is a small open portal in time.
Soon it will close. Mother's loving touch
will not go away, nor will a young boys play.

The vantage point will shift but
the picture will remain as will
son and mother......to one another.

THE FALLEN

The fallen one is here to deceive.
It's the key to his nefarious plan.
It matters not to him just what you believe,
as long as you just don't understand.

There are people who appear to be him
and the harm they do is hard to assess;
yet they only work in darkness, their perspective is dim.
He uses them to help make the mess.

His legions meet around the world
to speak of how much better it will be;
with their genius finally recognized
and all their plans in place
and they will all take care of you and me.

I have to say, I'm quite impressed
with how so many people are deceived.
How followers of Lucifer think somehow,
they are blessed.
It almost seems too much to be believed.

But then again, we've all been warned,
that one day all these things would come to be.
So now the prophet's words ring true
and we are in the storm,
until the King returns to set us free.

PLANTED BY THE WATER

There are no thoughts to share that reach
beyond the reason for sharing.
There is no charity of any value, if not from earnest caring.
There must be a beginning in all that people attempt or achieve.
The soul still cries for the deeper thing...something to believe.

Eternal flows the force that lives beyond the selfish realm.
Without beginning and without end, self can't be at the helm.
This is what brings seasoning to all the rest of being
and enables, every now and then the sightless, joy of seeing.

Winds will blow and rain will come as well as angry tide.
It may be much worse for some without an on board guide.
Look close and you may notice a light there in the eyes.
The ones who know eternity and now possess the prize.

The heart song comes in rivers fresh from the eternal flow.
The ones who have the music, have it well and well they know.
Desperation has abandoned them, they have no need at all.
Now they freely share the substance come from One who gave it all.

WE THINK, THEREFORE WE AREN'T

The most engaging thought has come and
danced around inside my head.
As I stood entranced and watched it dance,
I took in the things it said.
The thought was, life is lived until the day that which lived is dead.

Now, you may think, "are you for real? don't I already know?
What kind of person shares such things? You must be really slow."
All that I can say concerning this is, I know just what I know.

If one be now alive and later on be dead, a question comes to mind;
What need have I of all these thoughts here dancing in my head?
What reason I am now alive and waiting to be dead?

Perhaps alive and dead are here to drive a body nuts
and I'd confront the both of them, if I just had the guts.
A door has opened for a while and then it rudely shuts.

I'm certain there is more to know of this vexatious lot.
There has to be an answer, there has to be a plot.
There has to be a reason we learn when we are taught.

We watch the dancers in our head and wonder how and why?
The music may be rhapsody, perhaps a lullaby.
We look around inside our head but never to the sky.

INDIFFERENT TIME

It seems as though time has some spurious agenda,
with its moving on and showing indifference to all.
A moment was and is no more; no chance of its return.
We bid time please slow down but time won't heed our call.

In youth, we blindly squander, disregarding indifferent time.
Still, it moves on with apparent purpose and greater disregard.
We look toward another mountain, to plan another climb
but time begins to have its way and renders things once easy, hard.

Time, is the product of our own disobedience in the garden.
We were designed to be eternal and to carry on forever.
Now the curse that brought indifferent time our way
works to take away our dreams and make us believe in never.

THE LIFE I WOULD DESIGN

The life I would design,
Could never be Divine.
Too much of self would crack and tarnish;
Skins would burst and lose the wine.

The road I travel is not straight.
My purpose is not pure.
Still, I'll not be arriving late,
with God's direction sure.

When I hear the thunder roll
And lightening fills the sky,
I know that God is in control
And knows the how and why.

Though weak and feeble I may be
And fraught with human frailty;
I choose to trust the God who is
And all I have and am, is His.

UNITING LOVE

I know this: it is my purpose to write.
However noble or ignoble; it is.
If I am able to write in such a way
as to fulfill that purpose, then I am content.
I would like to write in the way that certain men lived.

These are men I would describe as committed and heroic.
They had differences to be sure but I know, in the
eternal realm the differences will not have or need any measure.
Each of these men knew, there were more heroic, brave and
deserving than they but to us, none more famous.

I believe that Abe Lincoln, Dr. King, Jack and Bobby
Kennedy, Dutch Reagan and Dr. Billy Graham all answered
a call and gave us examples of passionate commitment.
We have been shown strength and uncompromising loyalty
to justice and the power of human value.

As a people world and nation, we have so tried to
make everything about our party, our denomination, our
philosophy of government to the extent that we have lied,
cheated and stolen the character that men such as these
have for their brief moment put before us.

We have become woefully ignorant and painfully arrogant
in using these people to further causes that they were
so far removed from. Their goodness eludes us as all of their
enemies point out their weaknesses; as though the rest of us
haven't any.

Oh that we could see through our tears what Divine Providence
has so graciously arranged. These five men have done their jobs.
The thing that marks them, is their unselfish giving.
They did not endeavor to any parasitic profession or
to stir up people's hatred and or anger; rather they
gave and gave and all in different ways to full measure.

In my mind, I picture these men as friends seated around
a table, sharing the same love that motivated them. I know
that in another realm, it really is that way.
Tomorrow, when you go out the door, will you purpose to
take that same love with you and in every way you can...give.

HOW IT GOES

The dark calls out from its darkness,
"Men of wisdom bring your light."
The one who hates serves as sentry
and guards the expanding perimeters.

So one brings what is conceived in haste
and delivers only fodder for the critics.
The sentry wears a taunting smile
as another falls short of the mark.

Then, one notices the glow of silence
and finds a haven of refreshing within its embrace.
Wisdom, in the quiet brings her light.
The light gets brighter and drives back the darkness.

JUST ONE STEP

Just one step in His direction
and you will never be the same.
The very moment it is taken,
the Book Of Life contains your name.

The thief that died next to the Savior,
said, "Jesus please remember me";
then Jesus said, " This day I tell you,
You'll be in Paradise with Me.

Life on earth will still be trouble
but somehow you will always know,
Life eternal is your treasure
because of Him who loves you so.

By your own works, you cannot earn
or have what He does freely give
but if you trust Him, you will learn
just what it is to really live.

THE SADNESS COMES

The sadness comes....
when I think of all the times I had all the answers
and my opinion twisted like a knife in someone else's heart.
Having had my say, I would walk away and search
for other wayward ones to bring my shining truth.

The sadness comes....
when I realize my insignificance and begin to understand,
I am but a quark among atoms in a world teeming with injustice.
People have lost all they dearly prize in the name of progress
and the progressives prize only their ignoble destiny.

The sadness comes....
knowing that humans experiment on each other and no longer
have any sensitivity in their calloused souls.
There is taking disguised as giving and dying described as living
and people lonely and lost, with no proclivity to trust.

The sadness comes....
in the realization that I owe nearly everyone an apology
for being a voluntary, ongoing participant in original sin.
Even as the clock winds down, I revel in seasons of arrogance
and believe things long ago proven untrue.

The sadness comes....
when I have lost count of the times speaking and knowing love
yet there has not been enough to mortar the joints of humanity's wall.
No matter the depth of my understanding or, what might
remain of the sensitivity that is mine.....

The sadness comes

COMING BACK

The crying and the pain goes on;
more generations here, then gone.
Jesus whispers on the wind,
says, "I'll be coming back again."

The lies declared as truth, deceive
and many in their pride believe
as Jesus whispers in the wind,
"I'll be coming back again."

The devil's work intensifying
and those who buy the lie are dying,
while Jesus in the Rain and wind
says, I'll soon be coming back again.

The boisterous devil shouts his words
and empty promises again are heard.
One final shout and shouting ends.
King Jesus, has come back again.

THE L WORD

Love....The word we hear used so often and in so many ways.
Our understanding is so limited and we miss what it's about.
Love is meant to soften hardened hearts and brighten other's days;
not to satisfy ourselves and work our own fixations out.

Love, is patient, Love is kind and never after One's own good.
Love is God and God defined, as focused on those all around.
Jesus showed it to the world by dying on a cross of wood;
that mankind, from that moment on, would
see His wondrous grace abound.

Love is not a matter of the way we feel or how we're drawn,
rather it reveals in us, desire that comes down from above.
Love is the willful doing, as God propels us on
and nothing is more powerful, than His compelling love.

ON THE WIND

After blowing around, the note touched the ground,
to rest and await the arrival
of those who would read and there, in their need,
experience wondrous Revival.
It was written in love and dispatched from above,
to the place where the message is heeded ;
on the wind of the Spirit it travels through time
and lights where it's very much needed.
Where it will, the wind blows and it goes where it goes
and no mortal will ever hold sway,
for It's ever too dear and it's message too clear
to be handled by one made of clay.
So, we seek to find rest and in it we're blessed
as the Author so clearly intended
and we will arrive, ever safe and alive
right after this journey has ended.

TO KNOW AND DEFINE

The way of the Spirit is strange and puzzling to man.
Man has ideas built upon other men's words and persuasion.
Men have set about to discover and conquer, not knowing.
There is nothing of God that is conquerable,
though much to discover.

We are as elves attempting to bind Gulliver for our amusement.
He means us no harm, though we mean plenty for ourselves.
We know so little of His world and yet we speak incessantly of it.
This one and only great God speaks and we are slow to listen.

If we could remain still and silent, we would
begin to know our own need.
We are spirit beings, full of desire for spiritual connection.
Not all that is spiritual is good and we must learn to discern.
God knows and loves us. We need to learn of
knowing and even more so.... loving.

RESURRECTION DAY

The grave was dark and cold; surrounded by stone
with a silence that was undefinable and haunting.
The body of Jesus, resting there after suffering and death.
Now, it seemed His followers were for a leader now found wanting.

What a sad situation after so much love and hoping.
The Leader gone and all His friends left powerless and groping.
Oh! The pain of such dark days with all of the forgetting;
words of hope to take away the futile, blind regretting.

Phillip who said, "Show us the Father." had already forgot the reply.
"Have I been with you so long and you do not know Me?"
And what of the words of the prophets and
how the Son of Man must die.
His friends now walked in blindness asking,
"How could this thing be?"

Back at the lonely grave, with day's approaching light,
another light flashed brilliant; ending death's dark night.
The massive stone no longer there, according to God's plan.
In heaven, Hallelujahs rang. Out walked the Son of Man.

OH WHAT A SPECIAL DAY

The Prince of Darkness did his worst today,
convinced that life was something he had power to take away.
With cunning and deluded mind, he conspired to kill our King;
certain of the hopelessness, such a loss would bring.

I wonder if he understood the things that were foretold?
If he did, what was it then that made him act so bold?
Pilot, Caesar, all the Scribes and Pharisees were there,
conspiring to kill Jesus and completely unaware.

The prophets spoke of all that was and soon would be taking place;
and yet somehow the serpent prince endeavored to erase
the words that would for certain all soon be fulfilled;
That God would raise His Son again exactly as He willed.

And so the serpent's arrow traveled fast but missed the mark.
He was completely wrong about what happened in the dark.
This day a sacrifice is made; a way for all mankind
to enter into the Holy place and God for certain find.

TO MY GOD AND KING

I don't understand why the One who hung the stars
takes time from His doings to be my Guide and Friend.
Elohim Chayim, Adonai Eloheynu, The Hebrew God has
fulfilled His plan and secured for me, life without end.

Yeshua Ha Mashiach, His Son and the First born of many
is now my Saviour, my Brother, my Advocate and King.
With His Spirit alive inside me, I have all I ever need
and He gives me Life each day and reason just to sing.

I wonder at those who look all around and don't see Him there.
I will never understand the perspective they possess.
I have seen His Grace abound and had more than my share
and I will always bless the day I answered Him with yes.

So, To the God of all that is, I offer up these words;
knowing that they came from Him before I knew a one.
I thank Him for the life I live and blessings He has given
and look toward the day I get to bow, before His Loving Son.

THE ARRIVAL

Tell me I'm not here in total darkness.
There was still some light before I fell asleep.
Oh, I did sense it dimming over a long period of time
but my eyes were adjusting to the gradual change.

Who knew it would be as it now is? Pitch dark.
Now I am without any reference point or sense of direction.
All I am able to do is stumble and fumble.
Is anybody there? Somebody please turn a light on.

I feel a chill in my being that causes me great concern.
It's as though the darkness has come to stay.
Nothing in me wants to sing, dance or laugh.
I feel as though I've gone beyond the day of choosing.

I should personally be emitting light for others.
Instead I've squandered time, light and opportunity.
I should've understood the dimming and what it meant;
Now darkness is the reality that silently speaks.

SAVING UP

What have we taken from today?
Set aside and safely tucked away?
Something of value ever kept;
that we will have forever, come what may.

What is there, that is banked and ready there,
to keep our hearts away from needless care?
put aside for moments which we don't anticipate;
much like a timely, truly needed prayer.

What do we keep within our heart and mind,
insuring that we won't fall behind?
Experience and wisdom, always waiting in the wings,
with ears to hear and eyes to see, neither deaf nor blind.

PARADIGM SHIFT

How many times have you heard the word genius?
It seems such a popular word to be used in the
evaluation of people's lives and accomplishments.
We act as though someone has attained such a status.

Think about it; what original thought or idea have you had,
independent of anyone else? If you do possess mental acumen and
dexterity, what is it you have done to acquire it?
Are all of your abilities not gifts of either Providence or chance.

Have you ever noticed that you rarely observe arrogance in
persons of limited intellectual means? If we were aware of how
offensive arrogance is to our Creator, I wonder if we might not
value our brilliance in quite the way that we do?

I don't remember Jesus ever being impressed with genius.
I do remember Him saying, "Behold, an Israelite in whom there
is no guile "or "Among men, there is none
greater than John the Baptist."
Perhaps in our society, we could use a paradigm shift.

DO YOU KNOW WHO YOU ARE?

There is something around us, above and below us
that is at work whether we wake or we sleep.
It is the result of a loving call and so many believing prayers
and spoken affirmations that carry us from glory unto glory.

We have been blessed to come quietly into the Kingdom
as Jesus came quietly into the world we know.
Not many wise or noble with anything at all to commend us
and yet somehow, we are the called.

The wonder of all that surrounds, fills and completes us,
is more than we can condense into understandable dialogue.
The light here in our being is not understood by the world.
It is not meant to be. It is meant to attract.

Believer, will you consider what is the reality of your
redemption and the subsequent purpose God has given your life?
You are definitely His light displacing someone's darkness.
The realization of that should bring you to tears.

ROSH HASHANAH

The day or hour, no one knows,
The time the final trumpet blows;
but we were given ample reason
to fully understand the season.

The Bridegroom comes, with angel shout,
to call the Bride and draw her out.
The ceremony will take place
The Bride will look upon His face.

Then, the celebration long
goes on in glad and joyous song.
Messiah has redeemed His prize
and saved the Apple of His eyes.

Joined forever all in one,
Father, Spirit, Bride and Son.
The conquering Army comes to earth
to join Messiah's Kingdom birth.

Forever, it shall always be,
so many as there once were Three.
The lion lies down with the lamb;
protected by the great I AM.

PURE AND SIMPLE

There is a God and He has spoken
to the ones with ears to hear;
They are the humble and the broken,
to them, He will be ever near.

The proud will never stop to listen
to the voice that speaks of love.
They are too much like their mentor,
planning to ascend above.

There is no joy, when someone's losing
because they just won't hear His voice.
Still, it is an act of their own choosing;
There's no one else, can make their choice.

SERPENTINE STEALTH

The serpent stealthy and oh so cunning, crawls to
another place, where he might do what he does so well.
He is the one, whose deadly venom is delivered at
the conclusion of a deceptive long hypnotic spell.

The venomous delivery system, is one of arrogance and
hatred, disguised as some form of authentic concern.
Because of this venom and all its illusion,
millions, along with the serpent will burn.

Beware of the burn, welling up from within, projecting
the anger, damaged pride and resentment once buried deep.
If the serpent is about and no one protecting,
then your soul, could well be among those he will keep.

The antidote certain, providing immunity from all
that the serpent, in his grand arsenal may wield,
Is the blood of God's own Heaven sent Lamb.
If you are His, He will forever be your Protector and Shield.

UNIVERSAL IGNORANCE

As the telescope scans the Universe and the
many Galaxies are revealed,
people continue on in ignorance as though
the truth has been concealed.
The designers mark is everywhere; the signature of God
and yet believers in what's real are looked upon as odd.

The various observers, survey the vastness of it all
and with what's clearly evident, some still fail to heed the call.
There still exists the pride that separates us from the God of love;
even though we're overwhelmed with all that speaks above.

TO THE FATHER OF POETS

Often wandering, somewhere outside the poetry zone
I come to realize, it's not good to be here alone;
So, I find me a place where a keyboard is waiting
and begin to compose; thinking, writing...anticipating.

I do need to remember the power I've been given
to travel and explore as though being chauffeur driven.
The adventure of words and vast worlds barely thought
and yet written with design so cleverly wrought.

To the giver of this wondrous gift I do bow
for His loving kindness in knowing just how
to make it all work so that others will see
His loving workmanship, speaking through me.

SOONER THAN YOU THINK

When you wake up tomorrow, what will be waiting?
Will it be another day not much different from today?
I wonder if you know that great change is coming
and it is coming very soon, exactly when, no one can say.

It will be so very much sooner than any of us know
and when this change comes it will be easy to see.
It won't just affect a few of us but everyone there is.
This time of testing is even now coming right at you and me.

Only those who live in peace provided by the Master,
will have the strength to face whatever comes their way.
So ask yourself if you are ready for trial or disaster
and if you find that you are not, you better start to pray.

These things must be, King Jesus said, before the end will come.
Many here on earth are unaware of what will soon take place.
Earthquakes, wars and famines with people on the run
but those who know His voice will live to see the Master's face.

HEART CRY

People, let's don't study war no more
People, let's don't study war no more
As long as peoples need
is overwhelmed by someone's greed
there will always be another war

No one wants to take the narrow way
No one wants to take the narrow way
the problems that we have
will be here for another day
as long as no one takes the narrow way

Listen to the words the prophets say
God's people in humility must pray
If ever those of us on earth
would know a better day
God's people need to seek His face and pray

Tell me, who will stand where Jesus stood
Tell me, who will stand where Jesus stood
and put all that you have aside
for other people's good
Tell me, will you stand where Jesus stood

WHO'S IN CHARGE?

A story goes along so well,
then Someone turns the page
and breaks the long hypnotic spell
inducing grief as well as rage.

Who has time to readjust
when things turn around so fast?
It's as though we round the corner
just to face a shotgun blast.

Dazed and stunned by change that's come,
the quiet stillness teaches.
Afraid to move, we listen close
and contemplate the reaches.

Read on with caution, chapters change
and someone's turning pages.
Don't take for granted Who it is,
your rage and grief assuages.

This life you live is not your own
and few are your decisions.
The God who loves you, leads you home
by making His revisions.

WE ALL HAVE A MOMENT

Someone new is on the floor and now begins to dance.
Someone we have seen before in one brief passing glance.
It seems there's something different now, a purpose in her step;
perhaps it might have always been but, until now she's kept.

For this day is her moment and she's dancing to her song.
We all can hear the music and do so need to sing along.
This flower is boldly blooming in the warmth of midday sun
and her day is here for many years till all the dancing's done.

The orchestra of heaven plays while she delights the floor;
as all the angels watch in wonder, she Pirouettes once more.
Then comes the grand ovation, oh what grace and beauty rare.
This is the moment God prepared, for all of us to share.

WE'RE RICH

The salvation of God has come to so many of us
and He has settled comfortably into our lives.
It was not without adjustments in the beginning;
knowing that none of us were instantly wise
but, oh the joy of our days spent with Him
as our Captain, our Mentor and our loving Guide.
Where could we possibly go and not find Him there;
or where from His presence successfully hide.
We are surrounded by love and exceeding great fortune.
God's trust fund is there with abundance for all.
The Comforter fills us with warmth and assurance
and helps us to rise up if ever we fall.
No mansion on Earth compares to what's waiting
in Heaven's bright land when we finish up here.
We are rich beyond measure with all that's worth having;
a white robe, a gold crown and a Savior so dear.

THE SOUND OF LOVE

The sound of love is the voice of someone caring for
those who are beyond their reach but not beyond God's.
It is the prayer said believing that God will meet the
need of someone lonely, desperate and broken.

The sound of love is the soft whisper and the warm embrace
that arrives just before someone feels completely abandoned
and lets them know that hopeless no longer exists.
It is the sound of committed, Patient companionship.

The sound of love is a voice on the phone that smiles for
your heart and warms the chill of being too long lonely.
It is a teary eyed, "I Love You" when all that you are
able to think of yourself seems so unlovable.

The sound of love is the voice of anyone who will love
when they are moved to do so by the hand of God.
It is the sound that so many so desperately need to hear.
Maybe today, they will hear it from you.

A PLACE TO GO

There is a place that people come for refreshment
and it is never very far for them to travel.
This place is unlike everything else in their day;
and it allows them a break they so definitely need.

It's not up the block or just around the corner.
No, it's not even up in their room.
It is sanctuary certain in a time of despair
and what they've come to count on will always be there.

The place sometimes changes but it's always the same
always providing a refuge upon which one may depend.
It's not on any map but it's dependably there;
in the presence of a very close friend.

ORIGINAL INTENT

*Adam and Eve were created by God to provide Him
with fellowship and to provide them with all of their needs.
When sin came through deception and disregard for His
Word of instruction everything changed for mankind.*

*Mankind was now contaminated with self-centeredness and
became obsessed with accumulation and achievement.
People began to compare themselves with one another
and point out the others faults and failures.*

*As time went by people became hateful and murderous;
full of greed, jealousy, envy and pride.
This contamination continues to spread as the
population continues to increase.*

*None of this is what God wanted for His people but
it is what they have chosen and gotten.
Of course that is why we were in need of a redeemer;
so that God could restore His relationship with mankind.*

*Everyone who has received God's restorative gift
begins to see with His eyes and understand His heart.
God means for us to be in a constant state of rest and
to look to Him as the provider of all our needs.*

*As He works these things into our lives we begin to once
again experience Eden and all of its wonder.
In a physical sense, we are still in a contaminated world
but in the Spirit we live outward into that world.*

As we do that, the environment changes everywhere we go;
because where we go, God goes. He has taken up residence
within us and is living His life out through us.
If all mankind were experiencing this, Eden would be restored.

God will never write a final chapter because,
"Of the increase of His kingdom there will be no end".
There will, however be an end to sin and death
and the contamination will be forever banished.

God set mankind upon a pathway of freedom.
We took a detour and got very lost.
God has made a way for everyone to get back on the path.
His only Son is what it cost.

ROCK SOLID INFORMATION

The truth is etched in the rock of the ages;
Always there, never changing, ever true.
It rivals the works of the world's great sages
and speaks crystal clear to the fortunate few.

Only ears that can hear will respect what its saying
and the wise will take heed to its principles rare.
The narrow way beckons to wandering pilgrims
and offers all Heaven's great riches to share.

Chance meetings with fortune don't happen to these;
the ones who take life straight ahead on their knees.
They have a designer to plan out their days
and He's always there, watching over their ways.

His blessings come at them and fill them with calm
and the love He dispenses... a rich healing balm.
He blesses each day the ones He's selected
and the broken and humble are never rejected.

IF I HAD THOUGHT A LITTLE LONGER

Had I thought a little longer, when I was but a lad;
I might have finished stronger though, I haven't done that bad.
When wisdom spoke, if I had heard and learned without the pain,
I might have had more days of shelter
protected from the driving rain.

If I had thought a little longer when grand ambition came to call,
I'd have known a richer harvest, working hard and thinking small.
Some of what was long and troubled might have been another's lot
and I would take my rest more often, satisfied with what I'd got.

If I had thought a little longer before I spoke words I'd regret,
I'm sure I would have given others less to wish they could forget.
I know my life would be a blessing and my character much stronger
if many times along the way, I had thought a little longer.

THE SHADOW OF JUDAS

There are words hurled into the arena
by ones of diverse motive and opinion;
who have had their thoughts arranged in
such a way as to well persuade their minions.

Some speak of Mother Earth and swear that
she had all to do with our conception
and that she labored in our birth
ascribing phantom validity to their perception.

What of Eve? Is she not our mother still?
Is it not most like her we are? Do we not
lie, steal, cheat and kill?
If it's not true, why does He bear the scars?

Both Father and Mother determine the child.
There is no other truth of this.
Before sinful man could be reconciled,
the Master was first betrayed with a kiss.

CONVERSATIONS ON A PLANE

On some ethereal plane in times I can't design,
I'm engaged in conversation with long gone friends of mine.
So different and yet so much the same as it once used to be;
we speak of things so rich, entwined from where they are to me.

I am left in wonder yearning for another time so rare
when I could be with them again and fellowship we'd share.
I know that rarity and value are together by design,
so until we meet in Heaven, this rare privilege is mine.

SAYING GOODBYE

When we are born, for a while
life is about saying, "hello".
As we go along through our days
we find ourselves saying, "goodbye"

At first we don't say it so much
but as we grow older, we say it more.
While this is happening, we still say, "Hello"
but we find ourselves saying it less.

We say "goodbye" to people we love
as they make their departure from earth.
We say "goodbye" to our youth with
its faculties and do less of what we once could.

As age continues to come at us,
it brings more and more goodbyes
but somehow there is a lesson in all of it
designed to render us wise.

And so, we go on sharing, priming the pump
for those who follow, in the certain hope
that when our king arrives, we will say, "goodbye"
to this world and shout our glad "hello".

THE CLOCK OF TIME

The clock of time is winding down.
The winds of change are blowing in.
There are places that you've been
that you will never be again.

The clouds are racing across the sky
and with them war is coming too.
Then in the twinkling of an eye,
the one you serve will come for you.

The clock of time is winding down
and on its face the numbers melt.
Prepare yourself for feeling things
that before, you've never felt.

Those who recognize the tree
where blood and water brought them life;
will be the only ones who see,
their hope of glory, through the strife.

The clock of time is winding down
and sadly, many just don't know.
The great deception now is here
and they won't hear the trumpet blow.

A WORD OF CAUTION

Some of us are educated institutionally;
others, on the back side of the desert.
For many of us, it may be some of both.
The certainty is, we all need to be purged.

We have words in us that need to go.
They are words that feed our pride and
help convince us of our capability.
They are words that contaminate.

Whether or not we got them on the street;
Or in the classroom of some revered institution;
These words need to go because they continue
to create cancer cells in our being.

Your words may be different than mine
but they are most certainly poison.
I'll bet you can think of one now;
for others it's just a word, for you...?

Perhaps a high sounding word, not the least bit vulgar.
Maybe a word descriptive of your aspects.
When spoken, ears perk up and people take note.
So tempting to keep it and feed it.

Examine your words, which ones are your poison?
When a poison is introduced, swelling begins
but the venom doesn't stop there.
It is only satisfied when you are consumed.

Beware, learn to distinguish between the venomous
and the harmless. They are both; snakes, spiders or words.
Your ability to identify them will affect
your journey and ministry of life.

MARANATHA

No standards will ever be lowered
and nothing will change for the worse.
There will be no more need for a coffin;
no procession or even a hearse.

Mourners, we'll no longer have them.
There will be no more reason to cry.
All loss will be over, all pain and all death
and no one will ever ask why.

A new day is coming and soon to arrive
Messiah will come with a shout.
The sound of the Shofar the dead made alive
and those in the graves will come out.

Yeshua will rule and all will be blessed
of the ones who did choose to be His.
And there will no longer be thought for what was;
the Eternal is always what is.

THREES

Trouble comes in threes indeed;
bringing lessons that we need.
For instance, often on the fly,
they come with me, myself and I.

When I've finished fighting me;
myself and I will also flee.
Just when I think I'm fairly level;
Here come the world, the flesh, the devil.

The flesh is me myself and I
and so I know they have to die.
The world keeps telling them to live
with all the things it has to give.

The devil I work to resist;
he swears that he just don't exist.
I'm still a busy little guy,
just fighting me myself and I.

It's evident I need assistance
to continue my resistance.
Assistance comes in threes I know
and helps me as I onward go.

The help that comes is always there
to help me with my load of care.
The three who change my life the most
are Father, Son and Holy Ghost.

A MAN'S LIFE

A man has his hopes...his dreams...and his memories.
As he makes his way along the line between birth and death,
he begins to shift more of his weight away from dreams.

Everything changes, as only he and his kind may know.
The pestering urgency of youth has fled and is displaced
by patient wonder coupled with certain knowing.

He hears the roar of approaching water from up the canyon
but it produces no alarm. Its arrival is certain and there
is no hope of scaling the canyon walls.

He has the calm and the certainty of a promise.
"Yea, though I walk through the valley of the shadow of death;
I will fear no evil, for Thou art with me."

When a man's days are numbered, he is ever closer to their end.
No aspect of real truth will ever change, not even this one.
May we live out our years with the peace that comes from knowing.

WE KNOW THAT ALL THINGS
WORK TOGETHER

If you could picture yourself seated on a stool in God's workshop;
with God busy doing all that He does in keeping everything together;
and as you listen and observe and wonder how to be involved,
He looks over at you with a look of loving concern on His face.

Different things come into your life and His workshop;
things that He always uses with craftsman like skill.
Sometimes there is the pain of insensitive taunts from others
or the loss of a relationship through separation or death.

There are so many different happenings and circumstances
and they are all transformed into tools in God's workshop.
Some are used for shaping and/or tempering
others are used for very intricate minor adjustments.

We don't know which tool God will wield next, it may be sorrow.
If you examine your surroundings you may notice a tool in His hand.
You might just notice a word from a brother or sister
or a difficult circumstance in your life.

A gaze of concern from God may mean that he has to break you
so that in His own painstaking way He lovingly reshapes you.
It may be that He noticed an unacceptable and deadly flaw.
Hold real still, He loves you and you will come out far better.

Remember during these times how much God loves you.
If He didn't, He would not continue to invest in you.
Every circumstance in your life becomes a tool in the hand
of your most loving and kind Father. The result is always Joy.

BE VIGILANT

Be wary of you, for you can be trouble;
you can talk yourself
into doing things
that will cost you more than double.
Be wary of you.

Watch out for the world, it can be trouble;
It's full of people
who are full of games
designed to burst your bubble.
Watch out for the world.

Look out for the Devil, he's nothing but trouble;
he'll fill your life
with heartbreak sure
and leave a pile of rubble.
Look out for the Devil.

LOOK UP

The wars are here He talked about,
along with earthquakes and
famines;
Nations are rising against nation,
unleashing the forces of Legion.

People selfishly searching
for fulfillment of self in this life;
With everyone out for his own,
there's an increase in friction and
strife.

All talking of peace and security,
while seeking solutions from men;
believing they have the maturity
and intellect to cause the new age
to begin.

Children betraying their parents
and parents not showing the way;
Everyone angry and learning to
hate
while speaking of some bright
new day.

Knowledge increasing with
lightening speed
and people informed to the max;
ignoring the wisdom provided
by Him
and not surviving each other's
attacks.

The people of Jesus hated by most,
as they embrace the religions
of man;
Having no guide in their self-
loving host
and no viable salvation plan.

So it's down to destruction,
blindly they march
as they follow to darkness and
death;
and arrogantly swear to their
wonderful plan
as each of them draw their last
breath.

Jerusalem ravaged by Army
and Foe
this place that God gave to
the Jew;
though many would swear that it
just isn't so,
the scriptures declare that it's
true.

All of these things, with intensity
grow
exactly as Jesus declared;
He's coming back soon as His
people know
and those who are His will be
spared.

CONSIDER THIS

How much time is left to do
the things that are so dear to you?
Will there be days both long and full
to live and love and travel through?

Is it because you've planned it all
that somehow it will come to pass?
That standing, you will never fall
and running, never hit the wall?

What if this day were your last one
and your short race had all been run?
is everything as it should be?
if God should say, "That's it, you're done."

REMINISCENCE

In the course of living life
the rapid waters take so many away
people we knew and grew so close to
many we will see again, others maybe never

Sometimes I just ask God to tell them Hi
and in the process old memories flood my being
as I walk with them again and engage in conversation
about precious times of life gone by

Some day when time is gone and life goes on
a dramatic change is coming and all will be better
no more melancholy reminiscence or sadness
only the great sense of fellowship into eternity

TO BE CHOSEN

I remember being a child and preparing for a game,
we would form two lines and the designated Captains
would evaluate their choices and call out someone's name.

Those of us in line would jump around and say, "Choose me";
and the lines grew shorter one choice at a time,
until, all choices made, two teams did come to be.

The choices were made according to popularity or skill;
Because life is cruel like that and we form those habits young.
Being last or not chosen at all, could a young spirit kill.

If you have ever known this pain that makes one feel so low;
One heart identifies with you and all the pain you feel;
it is the heart of God the Son, the one who loves you so.

I have great news for you about the tears gone by;
God Himself has chosen you to be His own forever;
and as you live in His sweet light then no more tears you'll cry.

THERE IS JOY

There is Joy to be had in the realm beyond self.
It is always there, patiently awaiting our arrival;
When we no longer want what we no longer need and
turn away from all of our concerns for our survival.

When we embrace the death of our demanding desires
and experience life as it always should have been;
Then we will have ceased to warm ourselves by enemy fires
and God's pure light will warm us and
show us things we've never seen.

LESSONS FROM THE TOMB

I sometimes look for life in places where it's not;
and frustration leads me to remember things that I forgot.
Questions start to form both in my heart and in my head;
"Why do you seek the living, here among the dead?"

When the Disciples had arrived that day at Jesus tomb;
They forgot about the upper room and all the things He said;
The Angel asks them now a question always there for me and you;
Why do you seek the living, here among the dead?

Still I sometimes need to be reminded of these things;
as I travel through a world of paupers, lords and kings.
God's Lamb came to suffer, die and rise up from the dead
I should carry that same purpose in my heart and in my head

WE ARE BEING WATCHED

They are all in the audience, the ones who won't believe;
they are watching you and I when we don't even know it.
They see the way we deal with life and others we encounter;
they no longer want to hear of love, they want someone to show it.

Their arguments are subterfuge to hide their nagging sin;
They come in many forms designed to get them through the day.
So often close, the remedy is right there at the door;
the lost ones need a loving hand to help them on the way.

Please don't attack their heroes or criticize their sin;
that's never going to be the way to help them gain the prize.
Just let them know you love them and forget the negatives;
They already know what they all are, so we don't need to criticize.

Life is there to be the choice of everyone who will;
and some just need a taste of love to help with their decision.
So if there's someone struggling, let's help them up the hill;
if we engage in arguing we exacerbate the division.

PRIDE?

I wonder if you've ever said, "I'm proud of this or that?"
Some sort of grand accomplishment or maybe some new hat;
Have you ever said to someone, "come on, where's your pride?"
Or maybe just, "I'm proud of you" when you thought that it applied?

Pride is a word that gets used a lot with no great deal of thought;
of what it is or where it's from and from it, what we've got.
Both Heaven and Earth were perfect once so very long ago;
until the great rebellion that brought the world we know.

An Angel who was named by God, The Bearer of the light;
beautiful to look upon, became the prince of dark and night.
His beauty and authority in Heaven made him arrogant and proud;
He felt he could replace our God and that's just not allowed.

Then Lucifer was banished from Heaven's perfect domain
and cast down to the Earth below for ages to remain.
he is the fountainhead of trouble and it cannot be denied;
The fatal flaw that God did find in Lucifer was pride.

Pride is something, God has said that he intensely hates.
The problems that we have each day, someone's pride creates.
Humility and brokenness are what God loves the best;
And if we practice these two things, we will enjoy His rest.

THE EXCELLENT THINGS

We have the freedom and ability to speak of many things;
but before we speak we ought to think of the result it brings.
We can easily provoke to anger or hurt someone with what we say;
but if we chose our words more carefully,
we could improve their day.

What we might think of politicians, bureaucrats and such,
Is not the kind of information that brings a healing touch.
they may not know but Everyone is hungry
for refreshment from above;
and wouldn't it be special just to give them God's great love.

I pray that we will all be more aware of what we say,
and that we will speak kind words to brighten someone's day.
If kind words we can't seem to find as we prepare to speak;
Lord, then please remind us, silence is the option we should seek.

WISDOM CALLS

The undiscerning mind travels roads it should never be on.
In the morning it awakens to another hangover; another day wasted.
Sometimes the siren sound takes another mariner to the rocks
as he realizes his dissatisfaction at all he's drank and never tasted.

Wisdom calls out from her lofty perch and
as she calls no one answers.
The captives are all preoccupied with the melodies of fiddler's tunes.
Mindlessly they drink and keep their eyes upon the dancers.
Who minds the store? Why someone else; everyone assumes.

And then; another day has gone, expended in the vainest way.
Wrinkles form and eyes grow dim, the
fiddler's tune not half as sweet;
but his bow still strokes the strings as he now demands his pay.
This is the hour that always haunted; the reckoning no one can cheat.

THE LIGHT OF THE WORLD

Peace and joy are in the light;
when Love comes in, the light comes on.
In sin and hatred's darkest night;
when light has come, its darkness gone.

With its electric sort of flow;
Love is always ready there.
What those in darkness need to know;
is how much power we have to share.

As many lives become unfurled
and in the darkness grope about;
we have the power to light the world
and cast the prince of darkness out.

THERE IS LIGHT *(Hang On)*

In all the grayness and the rain,
I look to the west and way out on the water;
there is an approaching patch of light.
As I watch, the patch of light begins to expand.

The clouds are over me now,
as they have been for quite a while.
I thought the storms would never stop coming
but the patch of light looks even bigger.

Still the clouds are here, and yet
inside I feel despair being displaced by hope.
The light ever larger is creating
a glimmer out on the water.

As the sun moves west and the clouds east
the entire world appears to be transforming.
My heart is now filled with hope and enthusiasm.
The clouds are no longer able to maintain unity.

The sky has cleared and the sun is shining.
There were times that I thought that this wouldn't be.
I am consumed by warmth and light and my despair
has been replaced by joy and peace.

THE REAL ISSUE

We have been run over by religion from
the day some human thought he had the answer.
While we have played our sad and misguided song,
and our lives have been invaded by this religious cancer.

The issue hasn't ever been a doctrine come from men;
but we still practice long debate about who really knows.
The issue is the problem we all have with our own sin.
Our stubborn pride reveals it; truth is, it always shows.

The sin that separates us from our God and maker ever True;
and always there accusing us is Lucifer the fallen one.
Condemned to die, the sentence passed to me and you;
because of him, our lives are coming all undone.

Thank God, there is an answer that isn't from religion.
The answer comes from heaven, it's provided by The Risen One.
You cannot do one thing to save your soul, no not one smidgen;
Jesus died and shed His blood and rose again; the work is done.

CHANGE

It seems like nothing stays the same.
People come and go in and out of our lives.
Some act as though it's just a game;
abandoning their husbands or trading off their wives.

When we go into the store
to purchase what we always use;
it isn't where it was before
and so we search around confused.

Books are written about the way
we need to learn to live with change;
as if it were a wondrous day
when everything got rearranged.

This world is crazy as can be
as everything gets moved around;
it sure don't do that much for me;
though, I don't know what you have found.

Change is something I confess
of which I've had enough;
If I could straighten out this mess
then I'd be on to other stuff.

There's One I know will never change;
and that I know is true;
God will always stay the same;
He promised Me and You.

BEHOLD THE LAMB

As the clouds gather, we debate about
whether the storm is approaching.
As bondage is upon us, we speak of
unproven roads to freedom.

Life has come and now it is going
and we choose to go with it;
refusing to acknowledge that when
life goes, all that is left is death.

Our condition is grave and our
situation is bleak.
Our lives have barely begun and
then they are over.

There is no salvation in religion
and no hope in institutions of men;
but there is Life available, even
everlasting life.

Behold The Lamb of God Who
has taken
away the sins of the whole world.
He is building with living stones
what no man is able to build.

We should all become stones, we
should all join in.
It is a work of the Spirit; a
work of freedom.

Come and breathe the air of
freedom.
Come and know the Life that
transcends time and space.

Jesus the Carpenter is building
His church.
Not made with hands but
purchased
with blood.

Look closely, is this the One who
lived the perfect life?
Is this the One who is worthy to
be called The Lamb of God?

For you, only you can decide if
all these things are so.
But, things being what they are;
I would think you'd like to know

AS WE STRUGGLE

Life is going to be a lot of trials
and struggles. What we have as we
struggle depends upon choices we make;
What we decide to be in our struggles.

There is grace to be had and grace to
be given as we move on through life.
It is our choice to give and take it;
or to retreat into our world of self.

Our struggles may well be surrounded
by seasons of rest and renewal if we so choose.
Otherwise, we will be ravaged by fatigue
and unable to find the Joy of being.

These choices have to do with voices.
Which voices do we acknowledge as they speak;
The one that points out all that's wrong
or one who says what's right and good?

God, help us to listen rightly because
we certainly could use the rest.
Help us to listen to the right voices
and to make the right choices as we struggle.

THE FIRST WILL BE LAST

Kings and Queens, Lords and Ladies, Bishops and Cardinals;
we live in a world that vies for position and respects what is wanting.
We somehow believe that if we can attain
or at least know one who has:
That the sound of our own lonely unworthiness
won't be quite so haunting.

Perhaps we have forgotten Who created us
and why or maybe we never knew;
but we should find out before we die and this brief life is through.
The value of all people is in the reason that we exist;
Not in position or title or the fact you've made some list.

We should find peace and contentment in value conferred by God;
and not be consumed with resentment
when others might label us odd.
All of the valuable people, in humility find value in others;
Soon the lowly and the chosen will have many sisters and brothers.

THE POET'S PRAYER

*Lord, help me to write words that heal
and bring readers some joy and light:
help me to take them on a journey that
brightens their day or their night.*

*If I could take them down some corridor
they've never known before and when they stand
at a point of decision help me
get them through the door.*

*May they sense Your hand on their shoulder
as You speak to them through me
and if they suffer bondage
use my pen to set them free*

*Help me be there in their valley
let me share with them Your love
on their journey won't You guide them
with persuasion from above*

*When I think it's me, remind me
that it's Your great work gets done
and to myself please blind me
keep me to the race I run*

*It's for others we are gifted
so I ask You Lord this day
may some burdens please be lifted
by the words I have to say*

Amen

PEOPLE OF PAIN

The Hungry wonder, not knowing when they will have a meal
Widows in the quiet cold, struggle to remember what it was to feel
Somewhere, back beyond their now, they used to laugh and cry;
now the people of pain look deep in your eyes as if to ask you, "why?"

They march to war, our brave and young, believing all the way
but in the quiet of the camp, there isn't much to say.
Fair comrades fall in battles fierce and far too many die;
and the people of pain look deep in your
eyes, as if to ask you, "Why?"

The orphan wonders, "who and why am
I?" while drifting off to sleep
What father is there he can trust, his damaged soul to keep?
Do all the rules of love and life to this young waif apply?
as the people of pain look deep in your eyes as if to ask you "why?"

On sidewalks hard, in winter's cold, the frozen ones are there
waiting to be hauled away; life or death determine where.
Lives that ask hard questions that seldom know reply;
still, the people of pain look deep in your
eyes as if to ask you, "Why?"

STEALTHY DEATH

To feel the breath of stealthy death,
awakens senses long in slumber.
Who can know, is this the time
when God has deemed to call their number?

Taking all life has to give
and giving all you ably might;
right here in this moment live,
considering approaching night.

Again the breath of stealthy death,
reminds that time has limits sure.
What affords us squandered time
and detours caused by strong allure?

When stealthy death has come and gone
and one you cherish passes on;
Know this, deaths author is accursed
and weakened when he's done his worst.

May death to you brief stasis be
and vehicle to set you free.
May you take wings and know release
and may all that you have suffered cease.

IF ONLY

If only we could do life right
and always choose the way we should.
If only we were truly strong;
if only we were truly good.

If only we could see through eyes
in clarity, without the tears.
If only we could realize
that wasted days make wasted years.

If only we could take the hurt
and never have it make us choose
the bitter, angry, lonely way
and in the bargain have to lose.

If only we weren't human beings
with all the traits were handed down.
If we could have it all washed clean
and evil never come around.

If only we had ears to hear
and eyes to see the One,
who knew there was just no way
that we could ever get it done.

REASON TO HOPE

There is always reason to hope,
when you know who is really in charge.
It's not always easy to do,
with all that consume, living large.

Evil is loud and aggressive,
demanding to have its own way;
rude and ungodly obsessive
with hatred and vitriol, nothing to say.

There is oh so much reason to hope
when you know who will always be King.
Those from the dark side may call you a dope
but you still will have reason to sing.

AS NIGHT FOLLOWS DAY

The truth isn't lived, when the truth isn't known
and the truth isn't known, when the truth isn't heard.
The truth isn't heard, when the truth isn't spoken
and we live in a time when there's rarely a word.

Lies spoken often, that echo down hallways
and into the ears of the young and naive;
repeated as gospel, inciting proud knowing
and filling with hatred, designed to deceive.

We're one generation away from the goal line
when all will believe all the lies being told.
We're halfway there now and all that remains
is to eradicate wisdom and what's left of the old.

Good night planet Earth, for the day is far spent.
Night is upon us with the thief at the door.
So many certain, the night is not coming;
as the watchman cries out, they wonder what for?

A GOOD LOOK

Which way do I look, when things look bad?
Do I look back at what I once had,
or do I look down, for a direction to go?
Which way do I look? I'd sure like to know.

I need direction when all has gone wrong.
When I am weak, I need someone strong.
Do I look to my left, do I look to my right?
These questions haunt me, long into the night.

Which way do I look, when things still look bad?
Is there remedy certain, somewhere to be had?
Wait, now I remember; I know who I am
and so I look up and give it to Him.

I ONLY STAND

I only stand, from loving hand
that holds me firm and sure.
I am the one who tends to fall
but by the one who gave His all,
I am from His cleansing pure.

Any bit of me that is
worth keeping is because of His
wondrous change that's wrought in me.
Anything remaining bad
in me, is from this stubborn lad,
so resistant to who I ought to be.

There is no doubt that God is love
and daily watches from above,
with such great care, as all takes place.
All the work He has begun and completed in His Son
will be revealed, when we see Him face to face.

Until then, I stand by loving hand;
and not one bit by my own might.
I'm kept alone by God above
and by His endless grace and love.
He's always there for me both day and night.

THE LONG ROAD TO HIS HOUSE

On the long road to His house we quietly travel.
He never says much but He listens with loving care.
There are times the silence is broken by my curiosity.
He gestures, seldom speaking and I sometimes notice.

On the long road to His house, there are others.
Sometimes they remind me of me, other times of Him.
They draw alongside and engage in conversation.
Sometimes one will fall or show lame on the way.

On the long road to His house, there is always time
for the lame and the fallen and He insists they be tended to.
There are many along the road who are
not traveling in our direction.
They taunt and gouge at what they don't understand.

He doesn't criticize or react, He just gets quiet.
I don't know how I know but His eyes fill with tears.
My heart often seems to know His pain as if it were mine.
The talk of the journey and its end is bittersweet.

On the long road to His house, we've traveled quite far
and everyone is aware, our destination is near.
It seems as though more join us as we go; even more than before.
The taunting and goading gets louder as
we go and the travelers quieter.

When He does speak, He says loving things and tells us of His house.
It's hard not to share our excited anticipation.
We seem to travel in a state of joy mingled with sadness
and our hearts are broken for the sad state of the ones who taunt.

On the long road to His house, there are roses and there are thorns.
They tell the story of why we choose to travel this road.
Perhaps the critics and the taunters don't see Him because
He is in our midst and we obscure their vision. I hope not.

ANOTHER ROUND OF WHICH

Pray, which is mightier, the pen or the sword?
What is the yield that each wielded affords?

When bugles call out to dispatch into battle,
there is some effort required just to stay in the saddle.
And what of the blood that spilled, drains to the sand?
Is there anything owed to that death wielding hand?

We struggle so long as we reach for an answer;
acceptable, filling our need to be right.
The flames of the fire both warming and burning;
obscuring our vision with flickering light.

The sword, brings the blood and the death we despise,
yet, we won't turn away from its murderous lies.
Still the pen tells a story all written in blood
that speaks to its generous life giving flood.

Pray, which is mightier, the sword or the pen?
Both, by deception have taken folks in.

When the pen writes, no certainty brings guarantee
that the heart sending forth is in bondage or free.
Anything wielded by motives impure,
will yield bad results, though there's certain allure.

The heart of the writer shows through all his writing
and with eloquent style certain passions igniting.
Still, mere passion alone is no reason for trust
any more than glib judges will render what's just.

So we find that this dilemma has horns that are sharp
while dead pensmen and swordsmen may both play the harp.
There may be no answer in which we do wield,
rather, tracing the motive from inception to yield.

Pray, which be mighty, the sword, or the pen?
All is determined, where motives begin.

SPIRITUAL ECONOMICS

With each withdrawal from the wisdom bank,
there is more in your account.
And you'll have only God to thank,
as He increases the amount.

A TIME FOR BEING

When Lucifer was cast down, he was a proud Angel
with an agenda. His pride and Agenda cost him dearly.
God loved him very much and intended much better for him
than he chose but pride is very stubborn,
so he lost his place in Heaven.

People are either very much like Lucifer, with ambition and agenda
or they are becoming very much like God, full of love and grace.
We are surrounded with the effects of
personal ambition and agenda.
These things have brought the world society to ruin.

Nothing in our minds or hearts is more important than what's
important to God; Other people; every last one of them.
People of agenda will always sacrifice other people.
They will even do it, pledging their concern for others.

We now have a world full of that kind of leadership.
Self-important people of leadership who are full of themselves.
Such ones are the spawn of Lucifer, bent toward his priorities.
People of love are people of freedom. People
of freedom are people of love.

This holiday, I implore you not to think of religious agenda.
Instead, set your mind on God and the people He loves.
Be the you that He has planted and is growing
and let His light obscure Lucifer's antagonistic darkness.

VALUABLE ACQUISITION

When there is light, all who are not blind
are able to see.
For the ones who are blind, nothing changes.

Darkness brings little distress to the blind,
only noticing intermittent cold.
For the ones who see, night is a time to create warmth.

No one should be critical of the blind, only endeavor
to help them see.
Some who are blind will never see.

There is a touch that matters and brings warmth
to both blind and sighted.
We should all acquire it.

COMING AND GOING

If we had seen or could have guessed,
just who it was came knocking;
we might have ceased our roguishness
and all our vicious mocking.

We gathered well and ravaged better
all who in our pathway were;
not having much desire to fetter
ways so well designed to stir.

A new day dawned and found us doing
much the same as days before.
We gave no thought to what was chewing
on our souls, nor did deplore.

Building houses from regrets,
all planks and bricks that speak forever.
No bed of rest is there within
nor good is housed in this heart...never.

THERE IS ALWAYS HOPE

There is a sadness that comes over me,
when I see the direction of our world;
Yet, I knew it would all come to be
as things that once were, came unfurled.

Still the sadness lingers...along with the aching.
The blinded ones and deaf as well, neither hear nor see.
Some of them are my own kin and so my heart is breaking.
I do so wish they could live forever truly free.

It takes me back to Lazarus tomb, where Jesus stood and wept.
That vile and awful devil had Lazarus bound away
but at the Lords command, he could not be kept.
One once bound in darkness, walked out into the day.

There is hope in this vile and awful world
and we must always hold this great truth in our heart.
At any point in time or eternity, at God's command
The lame may walk, the blind may see and new life He may impart.

THE FINAL CHAPTER

*The Great American Republic is now in the rear view mirror
and as we move toward a future that threatens and promises
what it won't deliver, we watch the last images fade.*

*Our youth have spoken and forsaken their elders.
Wisdom now springs up anywhere it is declared to be so.
We have strayed from the ancient path
and chosen certain destruction.*

*Welcome to a Country without moorings adrift in an
ocean of Sharks. As our vessel deteriorates, they circle closer.
In our delirium, we will feed them and then, we are no more.*

*There is no more comfort here, there is no more security here.
The leaders are not trustworthy, nor the followers.
The truth has been replaced with the lie;*

and once more the Serpent speaks..."Ye shall not surely die".

A VALUABLE LIFE

God help us to follow the sound of your voice
and live out Your leading while we have a choice.
Grant that we'd seek You in all that we do
and as we move onward, to always rejoice.

May others be reason to give and to pray;
not some inconvenience that's there, in our way.
Lord Jesus your light and your love they should see
and hear it as well in the things that we say.

I've life everlasting, deserving of death;
so Lord I will praise you till my dying breath.
Still others need saving and being set free;
so Lord may they hear your great truth, if even from me.

ADAMIC HERITAGE

Struggle is not something I have chosen and yet, it is.
Being a son of Adam, I struggle by choice and by heritage.
I recognize, that I am both blessed and cursed;
still, there is always this longing for what was bargained away.

Oh, to be again naked in the garden with Eve;
innocent, alive and thriving with no pestering longings.
So much to attend to, yet without urgency or limitation.
Oh that we had not violated ourselves as well as God's trust.

There would then be days of pure contentment, filled
with undefiled purpose and life, always in the moment.
No need to plan or manage resources because supply
is always way beyond demand in fact, demand has never existed.

Now, the world is so saturated with squandered existence.
The sons of Adam still listen to the serpent and live the lie.
Yet all of the available evidence points to this great truth;
Being a son or daughter of Adam, you will surely die.

ASPECTS OF LIFE

Aspects of life give us light, encouragement and direction,
sometimes bidding us stay and at other times bidding us go.
Should we stay, we grow more and build
greater anticipation of the future.
When we go, we have the aspect of the past to give us light.

With the aspect of the past and anticipation we find encouragement
in knowing that one may steadily move from glory to glory.
Traveling with added light for clear direction, we expand our
understanding of why and better get to know ourselves.

As we travel, aspects present, taking their place in our journey.
One day the many aspects will be recognized as facets in the
Gem shaped by God's own hand, that has become our life.
No matter who you are, your facets are being prepared and revealed.

BAD TRADE

Serendipitous occurrences and occasions
are not explained because they often won't be.
People, not having any of that,
search for answers until they go crazy.

No part of just living, extracting the nectar,
is ever enough for the gathering mind.
It goes in the wagon; whatever we pass,
for we've no way within us to leave it behind.

We do it with people, possessions and more.
If we can't physically have it, it stays in our thoughts.
No matter how much we believe we can store;
a lot that we have, over time lays and rots.

We take inventory of all that we have
and all that we haven't that we think we should.
We wish we had time for the things that we love
but we've traded the best for what's not even good.

APPROACHING DEATH

The lighted candle flickers
as cold winter's winds come calling.
The short days soon yield to darkness
as snow commences falling.

What change has come so rapidly?
What cold has come, my bones to freeze?
No lingering warmth to comfort me
and no more dry, refreshing breeze.

The flicker of the candle noticed
and slow the melting of the wax.
Should this one yield to that which comes
and as it takes me just relax?

Soon, the answer to all questions
and in the morning, warm again.
At the end of this long evening,
comes the morning without pain.

THE OLD BRASS HORN

The old brass horn laid in its case for years, unused, unseen.
The metal had an ancient patina and had lost its early sheen.
It was never used and not abused, the inward parts like new;
still no one ever thought of it, or times they did were few.

Sadly, decades passed and generations came and went.
The old horn in the old house though much older, never bent.
Now, new people owned the old house and in the attic still, the horn.
A few short years passed by until, the "Gifted One" was born.

This young man was extra blessed, no vocal chords to speak.
An evidence of love so strong, providing for the weak.
The prayers of parents, friends and others in the town,
were heard yet waited for the perfect time to send the answer down.

A few more years and he had grown in curiosity and size.
As he explored the attic room, an object caught his eyes.
An old black case from just beneath a pile of things forsaken,
bid him, "come and open me" and he was somewhat shaken.

The "Gifted One" looked in the case and knew full well he'd found it.
This instrument would have a place. He'd build his life around it.
This moment in the attic is the one for which he had been praying
and gave him purpose and a voice to play what needed saying.

He cleaned and polished what he'd found and found it rare indeed;
For not a trumpet man around, a nicer horn could need.
He practiced long and filled his hours with disciplined precision.
The years would prove he made a good and very wise decision.

The concert halls filled around the world to hear the gifted player.
The old brass horn was always there, his instrument of choice.
The God of all that's musical providing answered prayer;
Providing what was needed to give the "Gifted One" his voice.

SMORGASBORD

We go through the line with our plates in hand,
selecting what's pleasing to later consume.
A dollop of this, two slices of that;
the selection is endless and so we resume.

Our plate ever fuller, we edge toward the end,
rearranging the things on our plate, adding more.
As we walk to our table, preparing to dine;
our plate is too heavy and is dropped on the floor.

Realizing we only go once through the line,
we work then, to salvage that which we have lost.
Sadness comes calling when we go to dine
because we neither have time, nor can cover the cost.

GOLD AND WISDOM

As Gold is found in the mountains
and in the streams that come from the mountains,
wisdom too has its place.

If you search for wisdom among the young,
you will surely weary yourself and mine
very little in the bargain.

A society that looks to youth, is
a society in great peril.
Great riches are forsaken in the pursuit of fool's gold.

The Elders are there, with riches to share.
Who will look and listen?
It is the dawn of our starvation.

FOREVER PERSPECTIVE

If I could choose a life where trouble didn't come, I likely would.
Then there would be no need for friends to rally around me.
I would not choose trouble, even some; It doesn't seem good.
If it wasn't for the trouble; when I cried,
who then would have found me?

Not that I'm in love with pain and seasons feeling down.
I much prefer the pleasure that I seek and sunny summer days.
Deep within my shallow brain are many reasons, I have found
to avoid the pain and take my ease in many ways.

Tell me what of grand design that always runs so far ahead
and what of God who by His love has shaped a future we possess.
He is the friend and so divine, not one of His, will end up dead.
Here and now, we look around to see who God would have us bless.

GOD HAS PREVAILED

Any randomness in life, was likely interjected
by disoriented man, who with sin has been infected.
God has a perfect plan, in ignorance rejected
and after all of that, man has still not been neglected.

There is Heaven, earth and hades and our residence in question.
No matter what we say, we have all been called to choose.
The world is full of voices and the power of suggestion
and should we choose our own way, then we will surely lose.

The blood of Jesus cleanses all who dwell beneath its flow
and do believe the one who died, their penalty for sin.
And for the ones who've chosen and His voice, they do well know;
the plan of God is back on track and we all live again.

RELIGION AND GOD

A religious man has his god.
A man of God is possessed by God.
A religious man has his standards.
A man of God is possessed by God.

A religious man has his pride.
A man of God is possessed by God.
A religious man must work for heaven.
A man of God is possessed by God.

A religious man has something to prove.
A man of God is possessed by God.
All men apart from God are religious.
A Man of God is possessed by God.

THE CALLING

Again, I wait for words to come
and I hope they are not just empty chatter.
I don't need words that come from me
but words that really matter.
Words that reach down deep inside
to touch the one who comes to read.
Words that anchor and reside,
meeting someone's deepest need.
Most anyone can utter words
and feed their need for much attention.
Poets ought to seek to bring
a more charitable dimension.
Somewhere not too far from
us, are those in dire need.
We should watch for desperate hunger
and always seek their souls to feed.

THE WHISPER

I heard a whisper in my ear
and at the hearing, shed a tear.
It seemed a message from above;
with words of sweet abundant love.

So soft and yet so full of power;
to fortify in darkest hour.
Twas sorely needed, then and there;
an answer to my pleading prayer.

I sit in awe with flowing tears
at how my King has banished fears
and thank Him for the many years
That I've heard whispers in my ears.

THE GREAT MYSTERY

The Heavens declare His handiwork.
By the Word of God, everything that is, became
and is so ably held together and in place.

What is man that he should be considered;
and yet, God has done this all for him so that
he might one day see his Master's face.

Consider the Ant, for we are so like him.
In relation to God, we seem even less, yet
God still loves us and extends to us His wondrous grace.

THE DEVIL'S ON THE HILL

It's another day at the park, with teammates all around.
The stands are full of people and their excited roaring sound.
The defensive team takes the field and warm-ups have begun.
You come out of the dugout and the coach walks
up and says "The devils on the mound."

"He hasn't got a decent pitch." the coach goes on to say.
"With all the junk he'll through at you, don't ever hit away.
He has a grease ball and a slider with a knuckle ball, you see
and he just don't throw nothin' straight. He's wild as wild can be."

The umpire hollers to the teams, "Play ball", you grab a bat.
Then you rosin up your hands and readjust your hat.
The devils on the hill and sneers, he couldn't be much bolder.
The coach reminds you, "Leave your bat securely on your shoulder."

The devil's catcher makes his digs behind you, telling you to swing
but you decide the coach is right and you won't hit a thing.
So, you leave your bat right there and you don't come around,
although, you're mighty hungry for that wondrous cracking sound.

All the devil has is junk and all you need to do is stand
and he will be defeated, it's the Coach's master plan.
The problem with the Devil is, he just can't throw it straight.
If you don't swing, he'll put you on. He can't get near the plate.

"Ball one", the umpire hollers; "Ball two, ball three, ball four."
Now you're headed down to first, the crowd begins to roar.
All those in Heaven's grandstands, know that victory's in the air.
They, everyone have played the game and done it all before.

Welcome to the big leagues, there are ball games every night.
The crowd is always at the game and cheering with delight.
To get out of the minor leagues, there's just one thing to know.
No matter what the Devil does, the Coach is always right

I AM

When the lost soul wonders at its condition and seeks for The Way,
The way is already there in the clear light of day.

When The Truth has made itself known to be true,
the lie slithers off through the tall grass toward the darkness.

When The Light arrives at the place of darkness,
it arrives without question for there is no darkness to answer.

IN CASE YOU NEVER HEARD

I wonder, now and then if there might be someone somewhere,
who doesn't know that they are the reason that Jesus bled and died.
There had to be a sacrifice for all our sin and selfishness;
one acceptable to God to set things right, so He was crucified.

The blood shed on that day was the price He had to pay
to save us from lives of empty selfishness and pain.
I hope you realize that it was God, in His
great love who made a way.
Now we should realize that any loss incurred is now our gain.

Friend, This crimson thread of love runs down through history
and shows up everywhere you look, if you have eyes to see.
Why God would go to all this trouble, seems such a mystery,
until you realize His great, great love for you and me.

King Jesus.... this life you have just won't
amount to much without Him.
Everything you do will leave you empty and needing more and more.
The important thing is do you know Him
and not just all about Him?
You may not care for what I say but, I hope
His words you won't ignore.

JUST INSIDE THE DOOR

As the sun breaks the eastern horizon, a new day begins
bringing with it bird songs and blossoms with refreshing aroma.
The morning air is brisk, though progressing
toward pleasant warmth.
As the sun crosses slowly east to west the warm has taken over.

This is a day as close to perfect as days ever come.
On such a day, troubles are more distant and life more sublime.
If only it could be bottled for future consumption,
on a day not so perfect, with all of life's trials and tears.

There is such a day in our future and it
comes, as the sun across the sky.
There was a time long ago, when there was no time.
There will be a time, when time will be no more.
It is the other side of now, just inside dear Heaven's door.

GOD'S WAY

Having taken more than I have given
and having more than I have earned;
I can't pretend that I've been driven
but there are many things I've learned.

If God's not giving it, don't take it
and stay untangled all you can.
Where you are going, you won't make it,
if it depends on your own hand.

God is a generous provider
and he loves to share his all
but if you're greedy and a hoarder,
your own portion will be small.

Keep your focus on the master,
take His blessings as they come.
If you give, they'll come much faster
and His grace you can't outrun.

EVOLUTION AND CHOICE

The clouds, white and gray in the sky,
offer assistance in my appreciation of blue;
like cataracts and floaters in my eye
that cause me to re-focus as I often do.

As senses dull and dwindle, still our sensitivity
seems as though it's growing more acute.
It's as though, if nothings lost then nothings gained
and without thorns, there is no fruit.

There is an evolution of sorts in this strange story
and it speaks of things with quiet voice.
We'll go from glory straight to glory,
should we make the proper choice.

A HYMN TO GLORY

The lamp once lit, has now gone out
and dawn is breaking, bright and new.
All that bound us, gone forever;
with His great glory shining through.

No more need of distance traveled,
no more striving to attain.
No more hopes or dreams unraveled;
gone forever all the pain.

Only Glory in the morning.
Only morning; no more night.
All together in God's Heaven,
where King Jesus is the light.

No more sadness, no more crying;
in that great forever day.
No more darkness, no more dying;
all that's evil, gone away.

If you've wished for apt expression
of the things you'd like to say.
No need or lack will ever hinder;
all is supplied in that great day.

Only Glory in the morning.
Only morning; no more night.
All together in God's Heaven,
where King Jesus is the light.

Life once lived with pain and sorrow,
death and dying filled with tears;
soon will vanish on that morrow
as well as all our doubts and fears.

When our Great God sets up His Kingdom
and banishes our greatest foe,
Joy and praise will fill our being
and his great peace, we'll ever know.

Only glory in the morning.
Only morning: no more night.
All together in God's Heaven,
where King Jesus is the Light.

Printed in the United States
By Bookmasters